SELECTING AND WORKING WITH CONSULTANTS

A Guide for Clients

Thomas J. Ucko

CRISP PUBLICATIONS, INC.
Los Altos, California

SELECTING AND WORKING WITH CONSULTANTS

A Guide for Clients

Thomas J. Ucko

CREDITS
Editor: **Tony Hicks**
Designer: **Carol Harris**
Typesetting: **Interface Studio**
Cover Design: **Carol Harris**
Artwork: **Ralph Mapson**

Copyright © 1990 by Crisp Publications, Inc.
Printed in the United States of America

Crisp books are distributed in Canada by Reid Publishing, Ltd., P.O. Box 7267, Oakville, Ontario, Canada L6J 6L6.

In Australia by Career Builders, P.O. Box 1051, Springwood, Brisbane, Queensland, Australia 4127.

And in New Zealand by Career Builders, P.O. Box 571, Manurewa, New Zealand.

Library of Congress Catalog Card Number 89-81251
Ucko, Thomas J.
Selecting and Working With Consultants
ISBN 0-931961-87-4

PREFACE

For many companies, there are clear advantages in hiring consultants for specific, time-limited projects. A consultant offers proven expertise in a particular discipline and an independent, objective point of view, with no addition to the permanent payroll.

There are also risks. You may have heard about, or experienced, situations in which consultants did no good or even made a mess of things. Some high-priced consultants do ride off into the sunset, leaving behind a trail of bruised feelings and recommendations that will never be implemented.

This book will help you navigate around the hazards of using consultants. Step by step, it will guide you through each phase of the consulting process—from deciding whether you need a consultant in the first place, to finding the right one for you and your organization, to negotiating fees and contracts, to building a productive client-consultant relationship.

If you are a novice, and fearful about using consultants, this book will reassure you. You are entitled to receive effective and fairly priced consulting services. This book will show you how to go about getting them.

If you are a veteran client, and completely satisfied with your use of consultants—congratulations! You may not need to work your way through every page of this book. You could pick up some useful tips, though, by reading through it. Try the ''Rate Your Past Performance'' self-assessment in Section I— there may well be areas in which this book could help sharpen your skills.

Novice or veteran, this book will help you to be a more knowledgeable and effective client, and get the most for your consulting dollars.

Good luck!

This book is dedicated to the loving memory of Lawrence L. Ucko.

ABOUT THE AUTHOR

Thomas J. Ucko is principal of Ucko Affiliates, an organizational consulting firm in San Francisco. He specializes in custom-designed programs to help organizations improve teamwork, communications, and leadership skills. He also offers workshops and seminars on dealing with change, consulting skills for staff and technical people, and on the subject of this book—how to select and work with consultants.

The author works with a wide range of clients, from large corporations to start-ups to professional service firms, He holds an MBA in management and an MA in counseling psychology. In addition to his consulting activities, he teaches in the master's program in Human Resources and Organization Development at the University of San Francisco.

The author welcomes your comments and questions. You can reach him at:

Ucko Affiliates
2 Bryant Street, Suite 300
San Francisco, CA 94105
(415) 541-0630

ACKNOWLEDGEMENTS

The following friends, colleagues, and clients made this book possible:

- Hillair Bell, Frank Carrubba, Carl Cheney, Cecile Currier, Aryae Coopersmith, Phil Edwards, Dennis Jaffe, Andrew Johnson, Margaret Nalbach, Mary Morrison Nur, Ken Petron, and Stanley Wachs contributed ideas and suggestions.

- William and Sue Miller and Stanley Wachs let me use their homes when I needed a place to hide away and write.

- Jim Kennedy of Management Team Consultants gave me concepts on interviewing taken from his seminar, ''Effective Interviewing!''

Most of all, thanks to Claire Cohn for encouraging me to write this book in the first place, and to Claire and our children, Kori and Daniel, for putting up with my periodic absences while the book was being written.

CONTENTS

CONTENTS (Continued)

SECTION I
WHY HIRE A
CONSULTANT?

What are consultants? The term can be confusing. It's hard to go anywhere these days without bumping into someone or other who answers to the label "consultant." And all these consultants are doing different things!

For our purposes we are defining consultants as individuals or firms with particular skills or expertise who are in business to sell those skills. They are paid a fee to accomplish a specific purpose, usually within a specified period of time.

THE CONSULTING PROCESS

The consulting process consists of ten major steps as outlined below and illustrated in the chart on page 4.

Step 1 The process starts when you, the potential client, identify a need within your organization. The need might be for information or advice, for a problem to be solved, for a system to be developed, or for new skills to be introduced to the organization.

Step 2 The next step is deciding whether or not to hire a consultant to meet this need. It may be more cost-effective to use existing staff. On the other hand, you may not have the right people in-house, or political considerations may dictate using an external resource.

Step 3 Once you've decided to use a consultant, you must define the objectives of the project. That is, what results do you want the consultant to achieve? What should be different after the consultant leaves? You must also specify how these results or differences are to be measured.

Step 4 You will also need to specify the type of consultant you need, and the specific consultant characteristics that will work best for your company and this particular project.

Step 5 Next comes the difficult task of getting the right consultant. This begins with finding potential consultants through recommendations and other sources.

Step 6   Then you must evaluate candidates—through interviews, reference checks, and written proposals—to make a final selection.

Step 7   After you've made your selection, you need to *contract* with the consultant. This means negotiating an agreement or contract on the terms and conditions of the project. The contract should be written and should cover not only the work to be done, the ''deliverables,'' the timing, and the fees; but also the roles you will each play in the project, how you will communicate, and what will happen if things don't work out as planned.

Step 8   Once the project begins, you will need to manage the relationship with the consultant. As with managing employees, managing a consultant means monitoring progress and giving feedback—both positive and negative. It also means adjusting contracts, expectations, and schedules to changing circumstances.

Step 9   The next step is what you will have been eagerly waiting for: the actual delivery of the agreed-upon product or service—a report, or an installed system or program—that meets the need identified in Step 1.

Step 10   Finally, with the ''deliverable'' in hand, you will want to evaluate the project—was it successful in meeting the need or solving the problem? You will also want to evaluate the working relationship between you, the client, and the consultant. What you learn from these two evaluations will greatly improve your chances of a smooth and successful consulting project the next time.

The Consulting Process

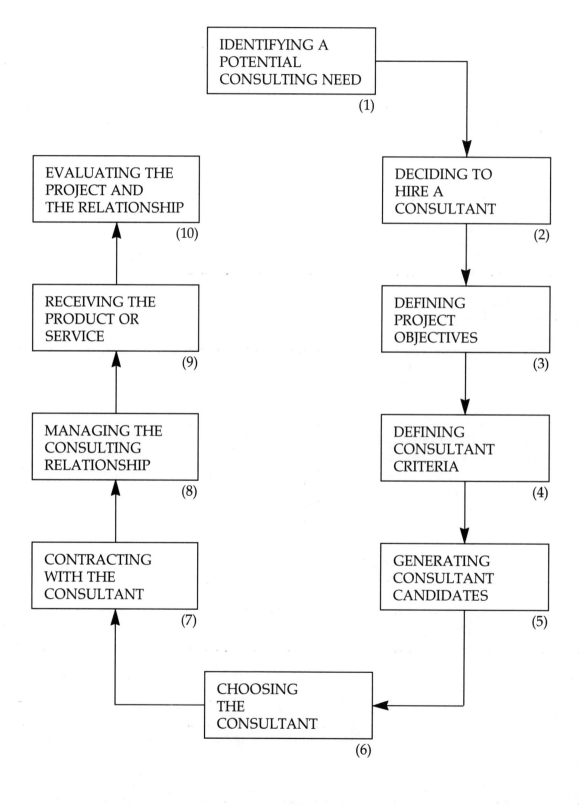

IDENTIFYING A
POTENTIAL
CONSULTING NEED
(1)

DECIDING TO
HIRE A
CONSULTANT
(2)

DEFINING
PROJECT
OBJECTIVES
(3)

DEFINING
CONSULTANT
CRITERIA
(4)

GENERATING
CONSULTANT
CANDIDATES
(5)

CHOOSING
THE
CONSULTANT
(6)

CONTRACTING
WITH THE
CONSULTANT
(7)

MANAGING THE
CONSULTING
RELATIONSHIP
(8)

RECEIVING THE
PRODUCT OR
SERVICE
(9)

EVALUATING THE
PROJECT AND
THE RELATIONSHIP
(10)

WHEN TO USE A CONSULTANT

Should you hire a consultant? Do you need one? Here are some possible reasons for hiring outside help for your project or problem:

1. **The skills you need are not available within the organization.** Do you have an actuary in-house? If not, maybe you need a consultant to help design your pension program, for example.

2. **Your in-house people don't have the time.** Even if you have the expertise for your project on staff, can your people afford to take the necessary time away from their regular work?

3. **You want a fresh perspective on your problem or business.** Perhaps you want the new ideas only an outsider can provide, or an independent, unbiased point of view.

4. **You may not know what needs to be done.** Consultants can provide an objective assessment of a situation and help define the problem.

5. **You may want a second opinion on in-house approaches.** A ''critiquing consultant'' can evaluate how well you are doing in such areas as strategy, executive compensation, or site selection.

6. **A consultant may be faster and more cost-effective.** Consultants who have done a particular project many times can often do it faster and more skillfully than in-house people, and sometimes at a lower cost (when you count the total cost of employees' time).

7. **When the project ends, or your business needs change, you can end the relationship quickly and easily.** With a consultant, there is no long-term obligation, or concern about ''wrongful discharge'' suits.

WHEN *NOT* TO USE A CONSULTANT

Even if all or many of the above reasons apply, it may be a mistake to rush out and hire a consultant. Here are some factors that suggest caution in hiring outside help:

1. **Hiring consultants can be expensive.** If you have some expertise in-house, even if not up to the caliber of experienced consultants, it may be more cost-effective to use your own people.

2. **The organization may not be receptive to a consultant.** Some organizations have a severe case of the NIH (Not Invented Here) syndrome. Others have been burned by outside consultant projects that missed the mark. Where the consultant's results are likely to be discounted or severely resisted, doing nothing, or getting by with an internal person, may be better than hiring an outsider. (An alternative is to use a behind-the-scenes ''shadow consultant'' who is not visible to the organization.)

3. **You or the organization may not be ready to hear bad news.** Consultants—good ones, anyway—tell the truth. Your organization may resist hearing about their own contributions to a problem you're hiring a consultant to solve.

4. **The organization may not have the resources available to support the consultant's efforts.** Consultants need staff time and availability to gather information or to implement projects. They may also need executive clout to clear political roadblocks. Where the right people at the right levels are not available, the success of the project is at risk.

5. **The timing may be wrong.** If the organization recently has gone through major change, it may not be ready for more right now.

MAKING A DECISION

Now that you've reviewed some of the pros and cons of using consultants, you are ready to decide if bringing one in makes sense right now.

1. What is the need or problem for which you might want a consultant?

_____

_____

_____

_____

_____

_____

_____

MAKING A DECISION (Continued)

2. What are the arguments for and against hiring a consultant? Check the items that apply, then add your own.

ARGUMENTS FOR	ARGUMENTS AGAINST
☐ Skills not available in-house	☐ Can be expensive
☐ Our people don't have the time	☐ Organization may not be receptive
☐ Need an independent point of view	☐ Not ready to hear bad news
☐ Don't know what needs to be done	☐ Resources not available for support
☐ Want a second opinion on our work	
☐ Consultant may be faster/cheaper	☐ Timing isn't right
☐ Easy to end relationship	☐ _____
☐ _____	☐ _____
☐ _____	☐ _____
☐ _____	☐ _____

3. On balance, which side weighs more? _____

_____

_____

4. What have you learned from this analysis? _____

_____

_____

RATE YOUR PAST PERFORMANCE

Use this checklist to determine how well you or your organization covered the various steps when you selected and used consultants in the past. Where your answer is "No," refer to the indicated section of this book to brush up on or learn recommended techniques.

In previous consulting projects, I or someone else in the organization did the following:

	Yes	No	Section
1. Evaluated the pros and cons of bringing in a consultant versus doing the work in-house.	☐	☐	I
2. Set clear and specific objectives for the project.	☐	☐	II
3. Prepared the organization and relevant staff for the entry of the consultant.	☐	☐	II
4. Ensured that key people and resources were available for the consultant.	☐	☐	II
5. Determined the right type of consultant based on project needs and organization fit.	☐	☐	IV
6. Developed multiple consultant candidates.	☐	☐	IV
7. Prepared interview questions in advance.	☐	☐	V
8. Interviewed at least two or three candidates.	☐	☐	V
9. Requested and reviewed written proposals.	☐	☐	V
10. Checked references on finalists.	☐	☐	V
11. Negotiated a reasonable fee arrangement.	☐	☐	VI
12. Executed a written contract with the consultant specifying expected outcomes, measures of success, target dates, and fees.	☐	☐	VI
13. Met frequently with the consultant to review progress and revise the contract, as needed.	☐	☐	VII
14. At completion, evaluated the project, the client-onsultant relationship, and what was learned.	☐	☐	VIII

IF YOU'RE A "BROKER"

How do you know if you're a broker? You're a broker if you've been asked to find or hire a consultant for someone else in the organization who will be the actual client. This is a common role for people in human resources departments.

It's important that you and the client have a common understanding about which of you will be responsible for the different steps involved in bringing in the consultant. Some steps, of course, may be shared. For example, you and the client both may want to interview consultant candidates.

Use this checklist to sort out which of you will take responsibility for each step.

Step or Activity	Broker	Client	Shared
1. Defining project objectives	☐	☐	☐
2. Defining consultant criteria	☐	☐	☐
3. Generating consultant candidates	☐	☐	☐
4. Interviewing candidates	☐	☐	☐
5. Checking references	☐	☐	☐
6. Selecting a consultant	☐	☐	☐
7. Contracting with the consultant	☐	☐	☐

In addition to clarifying your respective roles, you and the client need to communicate closely. For example, if the client takes responsibility for defining project objectives (step 1, above), you will need to know what those objectives are so that you can do your job in later steps.

Warning: Avoid the trap of selecting the consultant without client input. You could be the scapegoat if the project turns sour.

SECTION II
PREPARING FOR THE CONSULTANT

Suppose you've decided—at least tentatively—to bring in a consultant. Don't pick up that phone yet! There's plenty of preparation to do first. You may be impatient to get on with it, but time spent on preparation will go a long way toward assuring success.

OBJECTIVES FOR THE PROJECT

Your first step is to clarify your objectives for the consulting project. What is the result you want? Clarity about your objectives will help you to both choose the right consultant, and direct the consultant's efforts. To help you gain clarity, ask the question:

> "What do I want to have, or to be different after the consultant leaves?"

For example, you may want to *have* a second opinion or an independent perspective on some work that's already been done in your organization. Or what you may want to *be different* is a more efficient work-flow on your manufacturing floor.

Be careful to think of different end results. A particular tool, technique, or system may be a means of achieving the result you want; it may not be the only means or even the best one. For example, suppose your sales staff has been bringing in fewer sales. What you want to be different—the result you want—is higher sales, and not necessarily the sales compensation system or the new sales training program you think will produce that result.

This kind of thinking makes finding the right consultant tougher, of course. Focusing on end results may mean wading through different consultants, all offering different approaches that claim to produce the same result (in this case, higher sales).

Consider also "en route" objectives—goals you'd like to achieve along the way to your primary objective. In the example above, higher sales is your primary objective, but you might want a better sales analysis system along the way.

In addition to *task* objectives, consider also *learning* objectives—for yourself or others in the organization. Suppose you plan to hire a consultant to help you and your management team develop a strategic plan. That is your task objective. Your learning objective might be for the management team to acquire enough expertise to perform the task on its own the next time around—or at least to reduce the consultant's involvement.

Consultants with integrity will support such objectives, even if doing so works them out of a job. They know that their reputation, and word-of-mouth referrals, are worth far more than one extra piece of business.

CLARIFYING OBJECTIVES

Sometimes you know you want something to be different, but you're not quite certain what that something is. Or maybe it's hard to sort out the symptoms from the underlying problems. Here are some ways to help clarify your objectives:

1. **Ask yourself again: What do I want to have or what do I want to be different after the consultant leaves?** Review the questions below and check those that apply.

   ☐ **More information?**

   About what? _____

   _____

   In what form? _____

   _____

   ☐ **Advice or recommendations?**

   About what? _____

   _____

   In what form? _____

   _____

   ☐ **A new program or system?**

   What kind? _____

   _____

   What should it be able to do? _____

   _____

   ☐ **New skills or expertise?**

   What kind? _____

   _____

   Who in the organization needs them? _____

   _____

   What should the people involved be able to do faster, better, or cheaper?

   _____

   _____

CLARIFYING OBJECTIVES
(Continued)

☐ **A job or task accomplished?**

What results do I want? _____

_____

☐ **A check-up or assessment** to tell me what's going well and what isn't?

In what areas? _____

_____

2. **Bring together key people** who will be impacted by the consulting project. Ask them to help you define your objectives.

3. **Hire a consultant to help you**—ideally, one who is a candidate for the actual project. (See Sections IV, and V on how to select an appropriate consultant.) Use the consultant as a sounding board for your thinking. At the same time, treat this brief consultation as a work sample to help you evaluate the consultant for the larger project. Plan on paying the consultant for this work.

EVALUATING PREVIOUS PROJECTS

A useful bit of preparation is to review earlier consulting projects in which you or your organization were a client. By analyzing what went well and what didn't, you can determine what corrections to make next time and increase the chances of a successful consulting project.

Use this form to highlight key elements of previous consulting projects that went well and didn't go well. For each element that didn't go well, develop a strategy to correct the problem. A blank form is given on the next page for you to use.

EVALUATION OF PREVIOUS CONSULTING PROJECTS		
WHAT WENT WELL (and should continue)	**WHAT DIDN'T GO WELL** (and needs correcting)	**CORRECTION**
Project A 1. Good working relationship between consultant and my staff. 2. Project came in on budget.	1. Confusion about priorities. 2. Took longer than expected. 3. Problems with how well system runs.	1. Clarify and communicate to consultant. 2. Monitor progress more carefully. 3. Check references on consultants previous projects.

BLANK FORM AHEAD

EVALUATION OF PREVIOUS CONSULTING PROJECTS		
WHAT WENT WELL (and should continue)	**WHAT DIDN'T GO WELL** (and needs correcting)	**CORRECTION**

PREPARING THE ORGANIZATION

Bringing in a consultant can shake up your organization. Any doubts and fears your people may have about their jobs or themselves are likely to surface when they see you huddled in a closed-door session with a consultant. Do you think they don't know those are consultants you're interviewing? Unlikely. News travels fast on the water cooler circuit.

Here's what people may be thinking or saying to each other:

What are they up to?

How will this affect me?

Are heads going to roll?

Does this mean we're going to reorganize again?

Your job, when bringing in a consultant, is to pave the way for the consultant's success. That means allaying your employees' concerns, and helping them to establish a productive working relationship with the consultant.

The best way to accomplish both of these objectives is to hold a meeting with your staff, or with those people who will be affected by the project. Here is a list of what to cover at that meeting:

1. **The nature of the consulting project, and why you see it as important.** Tell them what need or problem this project is intended to address.

PREPARING THE ORGANIZATION (Continued)

2. **Your contribution to the problem.** This is the tough one for most managers and executives. But if you can be forthright about this, it will go a long way toward building trust and credibility for you and the consultant. This is also the time to talk about any changes that you personally will need to make in your own behavior for the project to succeed—and your commitment to do so.

For example: ''Our sales compensation system, which I designed, isn't giving us the results we want. We need a professionally designed system. And I need to watch out for my tendency to tinker with it. I promise to keep my hands off, and let the compensation experts do their job.''

3. **What benefit they can expect from the project.** Be honest. If there isn't any benefit to your employees, don't make one up. They'll know when you're not being straight with them.

4. **The resources you are committing to the project.** Tell them how much time—yours and theirs—you are committing, as well as financial and other resources. This tells them you are serious.

5. **Their role in decision making.** If at all possible, include your people in the early decisions that need to be made. This could include getting their help in:

- Setting or clarifying project objectives
- Deciding which consultant to hire

You're after commitment to the project, and there's no better way to get it than by involving people early on. ''Involving'' doesn't necessarily mean letting them make the final decision on, say, who to hire. But it might include participation in group or individual interviews, and listening to their input.

> **IMPORTANT:** Be clear with your people about the extent of their involvement. If they'll be making recommendations, with the final decision reserved for you, say so. Don't kid them into thinking it's a group decision if it isn't. They'll know the difference, and insincerity does more harm than good.

6. **Their concerns about the project.** This is a key step. You need to surface their concerns *immediately.* Unexpressed concerns may take the form of resistance, which can undermine the project.

For example, when new technology is being introduced, employees are often concerned about their inability to learn the new way of doing things—or about giving up expertise that provides them with recognition and self-esteem. Almost always, employees who will be interviewed by the consultant are concerned about confidentiality; that is, whether what they say will get back to the boss. If such concerns haven't been surfaced and attended to, employees may well drag their feet in supplying information to the consultant, give wrong or incomplete information, or try to derail or delay the project in other subtle or not so-subtle ways.

How do you surface such concerns? Try these steps:

- Ask; *"What are your concerns?"*

- Say; *"Other people in this situation have been concerned about _____. How is it for you?"*

- Say; *"If I were you, I would be concerned about _____. Is that true for you?"*

When people voice their concerns, you need to treat them as legitimate. Use your best listening skills, and then reassure your people. But don't let the concerns prevent you from moving ahead. Try the following steps:

- Restate their concerns: *"So you're worried about _____."*

- Share your own concerns: *"I'm nervous, too,"* or *"I'm also worried about _____."*

- State your determination to proceed, and ask what you can do to ease their concerns: *"This project is important to the company and to me personally. How can we go ahead in a way that's best for you?"*

Your people may not be willing to talk about their concerns. That doesn't mean they don't have any. Assume they do have concerns and do your best to draw them out.

PREPARING THE ORGANIZATION (Continued)

7. **What you expect from your staff.** Be specific. Tell them everything you expect. This might include:

- Information you want your staff to provide to the consultant.

- Specific ways you want your staff to cooperate; for example, providing space for the consultant, taking phone messages, or being available for meetings.

- Providing timely feedback to you and/or the consultant if things aren't going well.

8. **What your staff expects from you.** Ask your people what they want from you in this project. They may ask for periodic updates on the project status, openness from you, or a broadened role for themselves. To the extent possible, grant such requests. You're after employee commitment to the project; this is one way to get it.

Even if they don't ask, assure them of confidentiality. Let them know that any information the consultant gathers, through interviews or otherwise, will not be reported to you except in summary form—without revealing who said what.

SECTION III
ATTENTION:
BOSSES AND
ENTREPRENEURS

One of the characteristics of entrepreneurs—one shared by many corporate executives as well—is a strong need to be in charge, to be the boss. This trait has clear advantages. It certainly helps get things done. Employees will often sign-on for the excitement of working for a take-charge person who leads agressively. However, when it comes to being a client in a consulting project, that same characteristic can get in the way.

This section is addressed to those of you who are particularly strong-willed, who like—even need—to get your way, and who are used to exercising power and control to get your own way. Whether you are an entrepreneur, CEO, senior executive, or manager—you'll be referred to in this section as ''the boss.''

A SPECIAL NOTE FOR BOSSES

There are several ways that the need to always call the shots can be a problem. First, it can keep you from selecting the best consultant for the project. If the project involves an area of your own responsibility, or some aspect of the working relationships between you and those who report to you, you may be sensitive about a potential challenge to your authority.

WHAT BOSSES NEED

But, what bosses really need (at least some of the time) is someone to challenge them, to help them see beyond the blind spots that we all have. Needing to always be in charge leads to a tendency to avoid hiring the types of consultants (or employees, for that matter) who seem likely to threaten the boss's established ways or sense of control. When you fail to hire a tough, competent consultant, you lose opportunities for growth and change.

Even if you do hire a consultant who challenges you, your ''I'm the boss'' quality may cause you to argue, became defensive, discount the findings, threaten to fire the consultant—or all of the above. Most consultants, whether self-employed or working for a firm, are under considerable pressure to produce certain amounts of ''billable hours.'' Under such pressure, even a well-intentioned consultant may tone down his or her recommedations or back off from confrontations when faced with the threat—expressed, implied, or merely imagined—of losing the work. (Michael Doyle, a management consultant in San Francisco, defines a consultant with integrity as one ''with enough work that he can afford to get fired.'')

Being too much the boss can interfere elsewhere in the project. Suppose the project will ultimately require the involvement of others in the implementation phase. And further suppose you're determined to push this project through, even though most of your people don't think it's a good idea. Or that you've decided to hire a consultant your people don't want or like. How much enthusiasm or support for implementation are you likely to get under these conditions? You are far more likely to get reluctant compliance, or even resistance or obstruction.

Following are some suggestions for all you ''tough bosses'' when hiring consultants for projects that may impact your own decisions, management style, or role in the organization.

RULES FOR TOUGH BOSSES

1. **Be alert to any personal barriers to bringing in a consultant.** A frequent barrier is the belief that bringing in a consultant is a tacit admission of some weakness or failure on your part. Another barrier is the concern that by bringing in a consultant you'll be giving up control. You will need to explore these issues—perhaps with peers or colleagues. Even better would be to address these issues with the consultants you're thinking of hiring. That takes courage...but then you didn't get where you are by avoiding tough situations.

2. **Consider your own contribution to the problem you want a consultant to solve.** It could be an action you took. It could be passive—a failure to do something. For example, resentments among employees are sometimes traced to a boss's unwillingness to take action with poor performers. When changes need to be made, everyone, including the boss, needs to make some sort of change in behavior. Otherwise the organizational change will not ''take.''

3. **If you are willing to consider your own contribution, select a consultant who is willing to stand up to you.** How will you know this? One way is to probe for this in your interview. Ask for examples in which the consultant risked offending the client by offering unpopular recommendations. You can also probe for this when checking the consultant's references. If you'd rather test directly, propose something deliberately outrageous or unfair in your initial meeting. The consultant who accepts your suggestion meekly at this stage will not challenge you later.

   Remember, as the boss, you may have no organizational peers. You probably have precious few occasions to get straight, unfiltered input on your performance. An honest consultant who is unafraid of you can provide major opportunities for learning.

4. **Monitor your reactions when you or your ideas are challenged.** Notice any tendency to argue, get defensive, or deny the consultant's observations or findings. If you have the presence of mind and the courage to be open, share your reactions with the consultant. Experienced consultants are used to dealing with defensive or hostile reactions. The really good ones work to bring these reactions out in the open. If you can assist in that process, you will be immeasurably aiding the consulting process—and growing as a leader as well.

5. **Provide meaningful involvement in the project to people who will participate in the project's implementation.** This means doing more than asking your people to rubber-stamp a decision you already have made. It means listening to your people's opinions on such matters as whether the project should be undertaken, the best way to proceed, or who the consultant should be. Meaningful involvement does not mean that you must bow to your people's wishes; merely that you genuinely listen to them, and that you be at least partially open to being influenced.

THE SMALLER ORGANIZATION

The smaller organization is often a family-owned business, or an individual or group professional practice. In many cases, the firm will be headed by an entrepreneur, or by someone with entreprenurial characteristics. One such characteristic, the strong need to be in control, has already been discussed. Two other characteristics of entrepreneurs are: a tendency to make quick decisions; and a reluctance to trust others—whether outsiders or their own employees. Both traits can have an impact on the consulting process.

Another feature of the smaller company that has an impact on consulting is that such companies often have less money available for consulting fees in the first place. Business owners are also likely to have a greater attachment to their own money, compared to corporate managers' attitudes toward company funds.

The table on the facing page describes some of the pitfalls awaiting the smaller organization regarding the use of consultants, and offers some ways to avoid them.

PITFALLS TO WATCH OUT FOR

PITFALLS	REMEDY
Nothing new learned due to your domination of the consultant, and your insistence on your own ideas and answers.	Hire a consultant with the courage and skills to challenge you.
Reluctance to use a consultant even where it may be valuable.	Prepare, or have the consultant prepare, a cost-benefit analysis. Give the consultant small, trial projects to test the fit and to build trust. Get references from other clients, especially those you know and respect.
Losing employee commitment by not informing and including employees in the project.	Involve employees from the start.
Hiring the wrong consultant, due to an overly quick gut decision.	Use a blend of analytical and intuitive decision making. Force yourself to follow the selection procedures in this book. Insist on a consultant with relevant experience.
Bailing out too quickly if things start to go wrong.	Ensure frequent progress meetings with the consultant. Give early feedback.
Lack of financial resources.	Negotiate the consultant's fee as a percentage of savings. Stage the project over time.

SECTION IV
FINDING QUALIFIED CANDIDATES

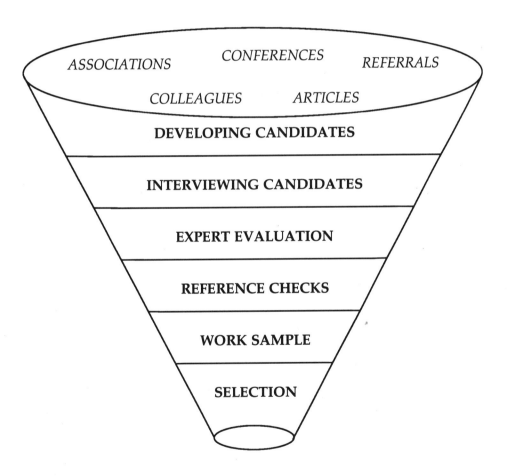

ASSOCIATIONS   *CONFERENCES*   *REFERRALS*

COLLEAGUES   *ARTICLES*

DEVELOPING CANDIDATES

INTERVIEWING CANDIDATES

EXPERT EVALUATION

REFERENCE CHECKS

WORK SAMPLE

SELECTION

Think of the selection process as a funnel. At the top are a large number of potential candidates, developed through the sources outlined in this section. In the next section, we will move down the funnel to arrive at a final consultant selection.

TYPES OF CONSULTANTS

Consultants come in all sizes and types. Sizes range from individuals to large multinational firms. The chart on the next page shows four principal consulting types or operating styles of consultants. It shows the service and ''product'' provided by each type, with examples. Each consultant type or style has been given a label that reflects the essence of the type.

The four types are not mutually exclusive. A consultant may operate in more than one style, depending on the project. However, each consultant will generally prefer and be most comfortable with a particular type or style.

Use the chart on page 29 to help determine the type of consultant that best fits your project needs.

> **CAUTION:** Make sure you select the type that best fits the project, *not* the type you're most comfortable with.

TYPES OF CONSULTANTS (Continued)

THE FOUR TYPES OF CONSULTANTS			
	THE DATA GATHERER	**THE ADVISOR**	**THE DOER**	**THE COACH**
SERVICE PROVIDED	*Information only*	*Advice and recommendations*	*Implementation of systems or programs, act as staff*	*Helping you do something better yourself*
DELIVERABLE	*Written report*	*Oral or written report*	*System installed or task done*	*System, task, and learning*
EXAMPLES	*– Market research* *– Economic forecasts*	*– Organization design* *– Selection of computer equipment*	*– Payroll system* *– Training program* *– Programming*	*– Management coaching* *– Team building*

Keep in mind that the "doer" may function in three different ways:

1. As an **expert,** telling you what you should do

2. As a **pair of hands,** executing your instructions

3. As a **partner,** collaborating with you

When selecting a doer, make sure you are clear about which of these three roles you want the consultant to play.

Once you've determined the type of consultant you want, you'll need to develop a pool of several candidates. Should you review all those consultants' brochures? Maybe. But there are better sources of qualified candidates. Here are the most helpful.

SOURCES OF CANDIDATES

1. **Consultants you've worked with before, or have seen in action.** Your best source of candidates is your own experience. In addition to those you've worked with, consider consultants who have impressed you at conferences or seminars.

2. **Recommendations from colleagues.** Call friends and colleagues—especially those you know well and trust—who have worked on similar projects. Find out who they used, and with what results. Attend professional or trade association meetings and buttonhole members. (You may not need to be a member yourself; most associations will let guests attend at least one or two meetings without joining.)

3. **Recommendations from other consultants.** Perhaps consultants you've worked with before are not right for the current project, but they probably know other qualified consultants with the needed skills or fit.

4. **Recommendations from colleges and universities.** This is a particularly good source of technical and scientific consultants. If you're looking for, say, a consultant with advanced skills in industrial engineering, you might call the head of that department at a nearby college.

5. **Articles in trade magazines.** Professional or industry publications will often contain articles about consulting projects. Scan recent issues for articles about related projects, and call the author or the publication for the consultant's name and address.

6. **Consulting associations.** Most consultants belong to associations. These associations will often give prospective clients lists of member consultants. Although this does not constitute a recommendation, at least you will get candidates who subscribe to certain professional and ethical standards.

Once you've developed several candidates, screen them over the phone. Ask them about their background, what projects they've worked on similar to yours, the results they've obtained, and how they set their fees. Set up interviews with the three or four who impress you most.

AN EASY MISTAKE TO MAKE

A mistake many clients make is to treat the interviewing and selecting of consultants as less important than the hiring of permanent employees. "After all," they think, "the consultant will be here only for a short time."

In fact, a single consultant may have far more impact on the organization than any number of employees. You've probably heard about consulting projects that went wrong and needed to be redone by another consultant—at great expense.

The cost of hiring the wrong consultant can be substantial. Don't fall into the trap of treating the process lightly.

> Selecting a consultant is as important
> as hiring permanent staff—
> and often more so!

DEFINING THE IDEAL CONSULTANT

Before interviewing candidates, you will need to specify the characteristics of the ideal consultant for this particular project and for your particular organization. Of course, it is highly unlikely that you'll hit a bull's-eye and find a consultant who exactly matches those specifications. But you're likely to come a lot closer than you would if you didn't know what you were aiming for.

Here are some factors to consider in coming up with your picture of the ideal consultant.

Writing your answers to the following questions will help you decide which factors are most important to you.

☐ **Relevant experience.** How much successful experience in similar projects do you think the consultant should have? A lot? Some? No similar experience necessary?

_____

_____

☐ **Industry background.** Does the consultant need to have previous experience in your particular industry?

_____

_____

☐ **Image, style, and fit with company culture.** What personal characteristics are necessary for a consultant to be accepted in your company? Should the consultant be reserved or outgoing? Easygoing or tough?

_____

_____

Does the consultant need to look, act, or dress a certain way?

_____

_____

☐ **Integrity.** How important is it to have a consultant who is known to have integrity in dealing with clients on thorny issues? A consultant who is known and respected by other consultants?

_____

_____

☐ **Location.** Do you want the ready availability of a local consultant? Or do you want the best, regardless of where you have to fly them in from?

_____

_____

☐ **Size of firm.** Can one person do the job, or does the project require a team of consultants with multiple skills? Bigger is not necessarily better, if the one-person firm can bring in other consultants as needed.

_____

_____

☐ **Communication skills.** Do you need a consultant who can communicate clearly and simply, or is this a low priority for you? Are you looking for someone who is familiar with your industry jargon?

_____

_____

☐ **Status.** Is the consultant's status a consideration? Do you need the reassurance that comes from dealing with a known quantity? Or do you prefer the dedication of someone who's still building a reputation?

_____

_____

☐ **Project goals.** Do you simply want a problem solved, or do you want to learn how to solve similar problems yourself in the future? If learning is part of your objective, look for a consultant with strong interpersonal and teaching skills.

_____

_____

DEFINING THE IDEAL CONSULTANT
(Continued)

☐ **Availability.** If the consultant has many other projects going, yours may get low priority. Is immediate availability an important consideration for you? Does the consultant need to have specific predetermined dates available?

_____

_____

☐ **Approach to consulting.** Do you want reports in writing, or are oral reports okay? Do you want something implemented, or are recommendations enough?

_____

Do you prefer a close working relationship, or will you accept a consultant who values independence?

_____

_____

☐ **Fees.** Do you have a fee ceiling?

_____

Do you prefer a fixed project fee rather than a daily or hourly rate?

_____

_____

Add any additional factors that are important to you:

☐ _____

_____

☐ _____

_____

☐ _____

_____

YOUR CRITICAL FACTORS

Review the entire list on pages 32-34, including any additional factors you added, and list the critical factors in selecting a consultant for your project, in order of priority. These critical factors will become your specifications for the consultant you want to hire. During the interviews, these factors will provide a standard against which to measure candidates.

CRITICAL FACTORS (In order of priority)
1. _____
_____
_____
2. _____
_____
_____
3. _____
_____
_____
4. _____
_____
_____
5. _____
_____
_____
6. _____
_____
_____

SECTION V
SELECTING THE
RIGHT CONSULTANT

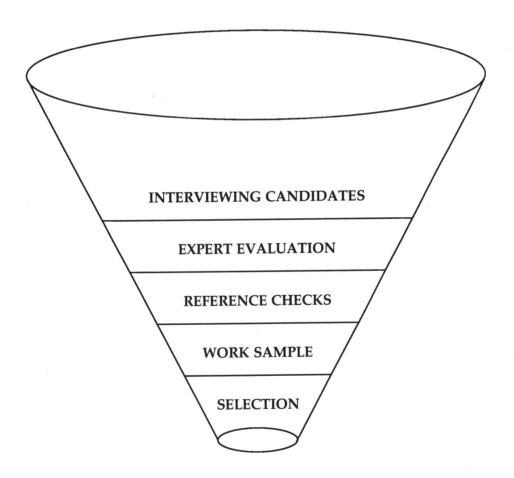

INTERVIEWING CANDIDATES

EXPERT EVALUATION

REFERENCE CHECKS

WORK SAMPLE

SELECTION

Now that you have a list of candidates and a list of the characteristics you're looking for, you're ready to proceed with the selection process.

This section will discuss the remaining steps as you move down the selection funnel from interviewing to final selection.

PLANNING FOR THE INTERVIEWS

The first step in planning for the interviews is to develop a set of questions you will ask all candidates. On an important project, you will want to have a number of people interview the candidates. This will allow multiple input on the candidates and will help to involve key internal players in the project.

You may want the group of interviewers to generate a common core of questions, around which individual interviewers can ask their own questions.

To guide your thinking, a list of suggested interview questions is provided on pages 39-40. Of course, you'll want to customize the questions to suit your particular situation. In addition, it's important to tell the consultant enough about your situation (being careful not to dominate the interview) so the consultant will be able to answer your questions thoughtfully.

SUGGESTED INTERVIEW QUESTIONS

Check the questions you want to use for your candidate interviews.

☐   1. What is your understanding of our needs?

☐   2. How would you approach this project?

☐   3. How is your approach different from that of other consultants?

☐   4. Tell me about similar projects you personally have worked on.

☐   5. Tell me about some of your successes. What is it about you that enabled you to be successful?

☐   6. Tell me about some of your less successful projects. What went wrong?

☐   7. How large is your firm? (For example, in terms of offices, consultants, billings.)

☐   8. What will your role be in the project?

☐   9. Who will manage the project? How much time will the lead person spend on the project?

☐   10. Who else will be working on this project? What are their qualifications and experience?

☐   11. What other clients are you now working for? How much of your time does that take?

☐   12. What types of information will you need to gather for this project? How do you plan to get it?

SUGGESTED INTERVIEW QUESTIONS
(Continued)

☐   13. What demands will you place on the organization?

☐   14. How do you propose to communicate the results back to us? (If not already specified by you.)

☐   15. Do you plan to get involved in project implementation?

☐   16. What are your strengths as a consultant?

☐   17. What are your limitations?
   Alternative: What would your detractors say about you?

☐   18. Whom else have you done similar work for? What results did you achieve?

☐   19. If I called them, what would they say about you?

☐   20. Is there anything about you or your firm that I haven't asked you that you think I should know?

Write down additional questions that will allow you to evaluate the critical factors on your list, or that will tailor the interview to your needs.

☐   _____

_____

☐   _____

_____

☐   _____

_____

If you are interviewing a technical consultant, and you want to test his or her ability to communicate well with nontechnical staff, ask two questions:

1. "What was the most difficult concept you mastered in college (or elsewhere)?"

2. "Can you explain it to me?"

A possible third question might be:

3. "I didn't understand; can you simplify it for me?"

The answers will reveal a great deal about the consultant's communication skills.

It is also useful to have the consultant interview with key nontechnical people who will be involved with the project.

MORE EFFECTIVE INTERVIEWING

Modest skills may be adequate for hiring job candidates. But many consultants are highly polished and trained to sell themselves. And as noted earlier, a single consultant can have a larger impact on the organization than any number of employees hire.

So there's a premium on good techniques when interviewing consultants. Take a training program in interview techniques if you can. It's that important. If a training program isn't practical, what else can you do?

Here are some suggestions to help you control the interview and obtain the maximum information from your candidates. For each item, note whether you already do it well, or whether you need to improve in order to be an effective interviewer.

	DO WELL	NEED TO IMPROVE
Create a relaxed and informal climate. Your object is to gather information, not to create stress.	☐	☐
Announce the interview format you have in mind. Don't allow the consultant to turn the interview into a sales presentation. Ask the questions you need to, even if it means interrupting.	☐	☐
Listen at least 70 percent of the time. You can't learn while you're talking.	☐	☐
Ask open-ended questions—ones that can't be answered in one word. Start questions with "how," "what," "when," and "tell me about."	☐	☐
Probe for and draw out the candidate's limitations. Ask why some projects didn't succeed, or the kinds of situations in which the candidate is least successful.	☐	☐
Draw out not only *what* a candidate did, but *how*. Asking *how* will reveal the candidate's skills, style and approach.	☐	☐

EVALUATING THE CANDIDATES

After each interview, you (and your interview team, if you are doing multiple interviews) will want to evaluate how well each potential consultant matched the specifications you drew up, particularly your critical factors. You will also want to evaluate several additional factors such as the following:

- **Personal chemistry and trust.** Do you feel good about and comfortable with this consultant? Do you trust him or her? Follow your instincts on this one.

- **Interest in the project.** Is this just another job, or does the consultant seem genuinely enthusiastic?

- **Is who you see who you'll get?** Did you speak with a salesperson or account executive—or with the consultant who will actually do the work? If you need a consulting team, who will be the lead consultant?

- **Concern for you and your organization.** Is the consultant sensitive to your needs and concerns? Does the consultant probe and challenge your diagnosis of the problem to get at possible underlying issues, rather than accepting your statement of the problem at face value?

- **Integrity.** Is the consultant direct and straightforward? How does the consultant talk about former clients and other consultants? Is confidentiality about other projects maintained?

A simple and effective way to evaluate candidates is to use a balance sheet, listing the consultant's strengths and limitations for each of the critical factors you identified earlier.

On the next two pages are two balance sheet forms. The first has been partially filled in as an illustration. The second is blank, and may be photocopied for your use.

SAMPLE BALANCE SHEET FOR CONSULTANT EVALUATION

Consultant _____   Date _____

Interviewer _____

STRENGTHS	CRITICAL FACTORS	LIMITATIONS
— Well trained — Similar projects	**1.** Relevant Experience	— none in our industry
— good at formal presentations — writes well	**2.** Communication Skills	— interrupts often
— good fit with most units — will get good acceptance from top	**3.** Fit with Culture	— fit with R&D?
— Small: we get his personal attention	**4.** Firm Size	— what if project expands?
	5.	
	6.	

BALANCE SHEET FOR CONSULTANT EVALUATION

Consultant _____   Date _____

Interviewer _____

STRENGTHS	CRITICAL FACTORS	LIMITATIONS
	1.	
	2.	
	3.	
	4.	
	5.	
	6.	

ANALYZING THE BALANCE SHEETS

If several people are interviewing candidates, each interviewer can fill out a separate balance sheet for each candidate. When the interviews are completed, the interviewers can meet as a group and compare their impressions (a flip chart is useful for this).

When analyzing balance sheets, be alert for sheets with no limitations. This may indicate the interviewer was not probing deeply enough. On the other hand, the appearance of limitations need not exclude a candidate; look for offsetting strengths. For example, a consultant may have never worked in your industry, but may be very intelligent and a "quick study."

WHEN YOU'RE HIRING A TECHNICAL CONSULTANT

(AND YOU'RE NOT A TECHNICAL PERSON)

To evaluate a candidate's technical expertise when you don't have any yourself, get someone involved who does.

The other person might be:

- A peer with another company
- Someone on your staff
- Someone you hire for the purpose:
  —A university professor
  —A respected expert in the field

CHECKING REFERENCES

Unless you have had previous experience with the consultant, it's *essential* to check references. (You wouldn't hire a key employee without a reference check, would you?)

> This is the one "must" about hiring consultants that is most often left undone. **Don't make this mistake. It can be costly!** Ask consultants for the names of two or three clients for whom they have done similar work, and **call those clients!**

Better still, track down on your own, some former clients of the consultants you are considering. Try peers at other companies or colleagues in trade or professional associations. That way, you won't get only those clients the consultants are confident will praise them.

Another source of references is other consultants. Ask the ones you've worked with before, even those in other disciplines. Consultants are often familiar with the work of their colleagues.

On the next page are some questions to ask a consultant's former clients.

SUGGESTED REFERENCE QUESTIONS

1. How did you like working with the consultant?

2. Would you describe the project the consultant did for you?

3. What methods, techniques, or solutions did the consultant offer?

4. Did you get the results you wanted? (Alternative: What good did the consultant do?)

5. Did the consultant complete the project on time? If not, why not?

6. Did the consultant stay within the budget? If not, what caused the overrun?

7. Did the consultant really understand your business?

8. How well did the consultant communicate with you and your people—orally and in writing?

9. What are the consultant's strengths and weaknesses?

10. How does this consultant compare with other consultants you've used?

11. Would you use the consultant again for a similar project?

12. Did the consultant maintain confidentiality on sensitive information?

13. Are there projects for which you would *not* hire the consultant? If not, why not?

14. Was the relationship with the consultant comfortable? Was it manageable?

Pay particular attention to how different clients responded to question 3. If the consultant offered similar approaches or solutions to very different problems, this can indicate a limited range, or a cookie-cutter mentality.

If during the interviews you asked the consultants what they thought previous clients would say about them (Suggested Interview Question #19), now is the time to go back to your interview notes and compare the consultants' answers with the clients' responses.

REQUESTING WRITTEN PROPOSALS

When you have narrowed the choice down to two or three candidates, you will probably want to ask them for written proposals. A proposal is a step-by-step description of what the consultant proposes to do (the ''work plan''), the results that can be expected (the ''deliverables''), the time span, and the costs. In addition, a good proposal will tell you the consultant's understanding of your situation, and how the consultant intends to approach the project.

The proposal won't necessarily be the final document you agree to or make into a contract. Most consultants view proposals as discussion documents and expect to negotiate changes or additions with the client.

Comparing several consultant's proposals can give you a great deal of information about their operating styles and approaches. You may have to pay for this information. If a proposal requires significant time or effort to prepare—for example, preliminary ideas on a new layout for your 25,000-square-foot offices—many consultants will expect to be paid for the proposal if they are not hired.

Review the proposals carefully. Also, invite others who will be affected by the project to review and comment on the proposals. Not only are you likely to gain some additional perspective on the proposals, you will be paving the way for acceptance of the consultant and the consultant's recommendations.

SELECTING THE CONSULTANT

Sometimes the decision is easy. You may find, for example, that one candidate stood out in the interviews, and that checking references and reviewing written proposals merely served to confirm your choice. Or you may find that one candidate's proposal was particularly well thought out and clearly superior to the others. Or merely that on balance, one candidate clearly has the edge.

Other times, you may find that a decision does not present itself so neatly. Two or more candidates may offer different but equally attractive advantages, or you may not feel confident that your top candidate is exactly right for the project.

THE WORK SAMPLE

If the deliverable for your project is to be a report, you might ask the candidates to show you reports from similar projects (with the clients' names deleted).

Another option to consider is to try out top candidates a small test project. For example, if you are considering two training consultants for an extensive management development program, hire them each for a half-day program on a related topic. Working with a consultant will make it much easier to decide if that consultant is appropriate for a larger project.

DO YOU ACT RESPONSIBLY WITH CANDIDATES?

Acting responsibly with consultant candidates means treating them with decency and respect—as if consultants were human beings with feelings, just like you! Acting responsibly means:

- Notifying candidates promptly if you've decided not to go ahead with the project.
- Getting back to candidates with your decision when you said you would:
  —even if only to tell them you need more time
  —even if you ask your assistant or secretary to make the call
  —*especially* if you've asked them to hold some dates for you...and those dates are getting close.
- Returning candidates' phone calls within a reasonable amount of time.

Acting responsibly isn't just the decent thing to do. It's good business. Do you want a consultant working on your project who's annoyed about the way you treated him or her during the selection process? Do you want consultants feeling resentful about you or your company—and possibly talking about it to others?

In the long run, acting responsibly with consultants pays off

---

SECTION VI
FEES AND
CONTRACTS

To be an informed consumer of consulting services, you need to know the basics of how consultants set their fees. This section discusses consultants' fees and how to negotiate them.

Before the consultant starts work on the project, you need to define the project, clarify what you and the consultant expect from each other, and describe how the two of you are going to work together. You need a consulting contract.

HOW CONSULTANTS SET FEES

FEE BASIS	ADVANTAGES TO CLIENT	DISADVANTAGES
TIME CHARGES • *When charging for time, consultant will multiply an hourly or daily rate (the "billing rate") by the actual number of hours or days spent on the project. For example, 12.5 hours at a billing rate of $100 per hour will result in a charge of $1,250.* • *Often, the consultant will quote an estimated fee or fee range in advance.*	• *Client pays only for the actual time worked on the project.*	• *No incentive for consultant efficiency.* • *Client may not know with certainty what the project will cost.*

PROJECT FEE
 	
• *On a project fee basis, client and consultant agree in advance on a fixed fee for the project, regardless of time spent. Consultants calculate project fees by:*
  1) Multiplying their billing rate by the estimated time to be spent—often adding a cushion—or
  2) Charging what they think the project is worth to the client, or
  3) Charging what the market will bear.
	• *Client knows in advance what the project will cost.*
	
	• *Less concern about consultant running up excess hours.*
		• *Potential for consultant to earn in excess of billing rate.*
		
		• *Potential for conflict if client requests services beyond scope of original agreement.*
		
		• *Potential for conflict if consultant underestimates time, then seeks to renegotiate deal upwards.*

RETAINER
 	
• *Consultants on retainer receive regular monthly payments. The payments may be in exchange for:*
  1) Recurring work, such as analysis of monthly financial statements, or
  2) Assurance of consultant's availability, or
  3) Discounted billing rates.
	• *Assured availability of consultant.*
	
	• *Often, a reduced rate.*
		• *Potential for overuse or nonessential use of consultant's services.*

Most fee arrangements will include reimbursement to the consultant for all out-of-pocket expenses. Many consultants will charge for travel time as well. Where full days are lost to travel, as on trips from the West Coast to the East Coast, some consultants will charge half their daily rate, on the assumption that they can get some work done on the plane.

BILLING RATES

Billing rates vary considerably among consultants, depending on such factors as:

- **Area of expertise.** For example, engineering consultants will typically charge more than, say, personnel consultants.

- **Location.** Consultants in large cities tend to charge more.

- **Size of firm.** All things being equal, large firms will generally charge more than small firms or individual practitioners.

- **Amount of experience.** The more experience, of course, the higher the rate.

- **Reputation and image.** A best-selling book, for example, will shoot a consultant's rates skyward.

- **Chutzpah.** The boldness or brass with which the consultant approaches the fee setting.

Actual daily billing rates for full-time professional consultants vary considerably. They may range from $400 or $500 per day at the low end, to $2,000 to $3,000 per day or more at the upper end—and substantially higher for the big-name ''superstars.''

In larger firms, the billing rates of the individual consultants are calculated from their salaries. A consultant with an annual salary of, say $75,000 might be expected to devote 1,500 hours during the year to billable client work. (The remaining hours would be spent on business development, administrative work, education, vacations, and other non-billable activities.) To determine the billing rate, the salary of $75,000 would be divided by the 1,500 hours to arrive at $50 per hour. This figure would then be multiplied by a factor of three or so to cover the firm's office space, administrative costs, employee benefits, and other overhead costs, as well as the firm's profits. The $75,000 per year consultant would thus be billed to clients at $150 per hour or $1,200 per day.

WHICH FEE ARRANGEMENT IS BEST

Here are some factors to consider when exploring fee arrangements:

- **How well defined is the project?** If your project is vague or unstructured, consultants will not be able to estimate it accurately, and therefore not work on a project fee (or fixed fee) basis.

- **Are you willing to take a risk?** On a time charges or daily rate basis, you are taking a risk; the fee may turn out to be either higher or lower than estimated. A project fee contract will limit your risk—but offers no savings if the consultant is highly efficient.

- **How important is quality?** If quality is critical, a daily rate arrangement may be preferable. This way, the consultant won't be tempted to cut corners if the project turns out to be more complex than anticipated.

NEGOTIATING FEES

Consulting fees are often negotiable. Here are some recommendations for negotiating fees:

1. **Know your budget.** Determine in advance how much you can afford or are willing to pay for the project, and tell the consultant. Knowing you have a fixed budget will often encourage the consultant to pare the project down to its essentials. But recognize that there are trade-offs. As with most purchases, when buying consulting services you generally get what you pay for.

2. **Tell candidates the importance of cost to your decision.** You will undoubtedly be considering various factors when evaluating consultants and consulting proposals: consultant experience, reputation, firm size, and so on. If cost is a major factor as well, let candidates know that. If you can, tell them how much cost will weigh in your decision relative to the other factors you are considering. This will encourage competitive quotes.

3. **Ask for discounts.** Consultants are often willing to give discounts from their standard rates for large projects or for work that continues over several months. Many consultants who are starting out will give discounts to build business. Others may consider discounts for various reasons: they find your project fun or interesting; they see an opportunity for new learning; or they want to add your firm to their client list.

   The discount may take two forms: less money for the originally proposed work, or more work for the same money. You won't always get a discount, especially from busy, established consultants, but it can't hurt to ask.

4. **Don't dwell on the consultant's fees relative to your salary.** This can be a trap. Sure, when you multiply a consultant's daily rate by the number of working days in the year, you're likely to get a rather high number. Your own salary may seem anemic by comparison, and you may resent the consultant charging so much—particularly if he or she is an independent. This can impair your working relationship with the consultant, as well as your attitude toward fee negotiations.

THE CONSULTING CONTRACT

A clear contract is the foundation of a successful consulting project. As in any relationship, when things go wrong, it's often because of unmet—and usually unexpressed—expectations. When experienced organizational consultants were asked about their consulting failures, an overwhelming majority attributed lack of success to unclear or inadequate contracts between themselves and their clients.

The contract need not be complicated. A letter outlining what each of you will do, and signed by both you and the consultant, is often sufficient. But your organization's legal or purchasing departments may have contractual requirements, such as nondisclosure agreements, which can add to the complexity of the contract.

The consultant's written proposal often forms the basis for the contract. But don't make the mistake of accepting the consultant's initial proposal as your final contract. (Consultants will often include a space for you to sign at the bottom of their proposals. When you do, this becomes the contract.) You should treat the proposal as a discussion document which, after your input, can form the basis of the contract. Or you can take the initiative and draft a letter of agreement yourself.

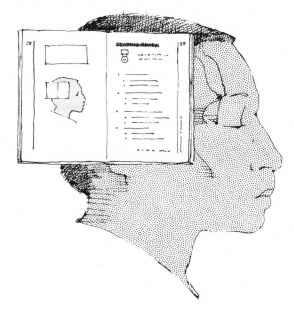

WHAT TO INCLUDE IN THE CONTRACT

Here is a list of items that have proven useful in consulting contracts. Check those items you want to include in your contract.

☐ **Term.** When will the agreement take effect? When will it end?

☐ **Objectives.** The results you want. After the consultant leaves, what should you have, or what should be different?

☐ **Definition of success.** What is success, and how is it to be measured? What is the standard of measurement to be used? Who will do the measuring? When?

☐ **Scope of the project.** The workplan. Step by step, exactly what tasks and activities will the consultant perform to achieve the desired objectives?

☐ **Deliverable or "product."** What will the consultant leave behind? A working system? A detailed written report? An oral report? Will there be a formal presentation? When are interim and final reports due? Will the consultant assist in implementing the recommendations, or is that up to you? Will the consultant provide ongoing maintenance to a delivered system?

☐ **Ownership of the product.** Sometimes the consultant's product has commercial value; for example, a custom-designed training program. Who will own the copyright? Will the consultant be able to sell the same program to other clients? Can you use the program indefinitely? Can you use it with other company units?

WHAT TO INCLUDE IN THE CONTRACT (Continued)

☐ **Confidentiality.** Consultants will often have access to confidential or proprietary information. If this is the case, you will want the consultant to agree to not disclose such information to others.

☐ **Communications.** What forms of communication do you want with or from the consultant? Periodic phone calls or meetings? Written progress reports? Formal reviews? How often?

☐ **Staffing.** Who specifically will work on your project? Are substitutions permitted? Under what circumstances?

☐ **Supervision of the consultant.** Who will supervise the consultant or be the consultant's primary contact?

☐ **Scheduling.** When will the project start? Are there dates by which on-the-way "milestones" are to be reached? What is the expected completion date?

☐ **Fees and payments.** Will the consultant receive a daily or hourly rate, a fixed project fee, or a monthly retainer? Will a portion of the fee be paid in advance? On a lengthy project, will payments be made at scheduled intervals, or upon achievement of specified interim targets?

☐ **Incentives and penalties.** Will there be financial incentives for the consultant to bring in the project ahead of schedule? Will there be penalties for running late?

☐ **Termination.** What if things don't work out as planned? It's helpful to agree in advance on how to end the contract if either of you becomes unhappy with the relationship or the progress of the project. How much notice must either party give? What fees will be due?

☐ **Cancellation policy.** What if the project gets cancelled before it begins? The consultant may expect compensation for days which have been reserved for you, and cannot easily be ''sold'' on short notice.

☐ **Arbitration.** If disputes arise over deliverables, fees, or other contract items, how will they be resolved? Often, the parties will agree in advance to refer such disputes to the American Arbitration Association or similar organization for binding arbitration.

Add any additional items that are important for your situation or your project:

☐ _____

_____

☐ _____

_____

☐ _____

_____

BEYOND THE WRITTEN CONTRACT

There is more to contracting than defining the nuts and bolts of how the project will proceed. There may be expectations that you and the consultant have of each other that seem out of place in a written agreement, but that need to be addressed.

In fact, the essence of contracting is the contracting meeting, at which your and the consultant's needs are expressed and negotiated. Here are some key issues about which you may want to agree with the consultant:

☐ **Feedback.** Consultants are in a position to give you feedback about your management or communications style that your people may not dare to voice. Contracting with a consultant for such feedback can provide significant opportunity for learning.

☐ **Communications.** You may want the consultant to give you weekly telephone updates or memos on project status. Perhaps you want him or her to brief your staff periodically. The contracting meeting is the time to raise such needs.

☐ **Consultant expectations.** Experienced consultants will generally tell you in advance what they need and want from you. If your consultant doesn't, ask. You will want to agree on the time, effort, resources, and access to people required of you and your staff.

SECTION VII
THE CONSULTING
RELATIONSHIP

A successful consulting project is a collaboration between client and consultant. When you and your people support the consultant's efforts, everyone wins.

SUPPORTING THE CONSULTANT'S EFFORTS

Here are several important ways you and your staff can assist the consultant in being successful.

INTRODUCE CONSULTANT TO ALL RELEVANT PERSONNEL

At the beginning of the project, make certain you have introduced the consultant to your reporting managers, to your administrative staff, and to any other people the consulant will need to work with or get information from.

APPOINT PROJECT MANAGER OR LIAISON PERSON

If you will not be overseeing the consultant on a day-to-day basis, appoint someone in your organization who will. Many projects go over budget because no one was monitoring the consultant's efforts closely enough. Try not to appoint a committee to this role. If you must appoint a committee, make sure a single person on the committee is charged with communicating with the consultant. To ensure that the consultant receives one set of consistent signals.

The project manager should be of sufficient rank or influence in the organization to send a signal that the project is important. In addition, he or she should be politically astute, and should be capable of making routine decisions or taking action independently. For example, the project manager should be able to authorize additional expenditures, schedule appointments with other staff, and offer the consultant advice on handling difficult situations.

This same individual can also monitor the consultant's progress and give the consultant feedback, in your absence. Naturally, you must ensure that the project manager has enough time available to do the job right. This may require a temporary transfer of other responsibilities.

INFORM CONSULTANT ON POLITICAL ISSUES

Political considerations are realities of organizational life. Ignoring them won't make them disappear. To ensure your consultant doesn't stumble, provide a roadmap of the political obstacles he or she may encounter during the project.

PROVIDE ACCESS TO HIGHER ORGANIZATIONAL LEVELS

If you are not at the top of your organization, and the consultant will need to deal with people at higher levels, make certain the consultant has that access.

PROVIDE SPACE AND EQUIPMENT

Consultants who spend considerable time at your location will need a place to work—office or cubicle, desk, and chair—and access to telephone and office supplies. Depending on the nature of the project, privacy may be important.

PAY INVOICES PROMPTLY

Delay in paying the consultant's invoices suggests that the consultant's work is unimportant. The danger, of course, is that the consultant may also treat the work as unimportant. Why take a chance on reducing the consultant's enthusiasm and motivation?

DON'T PILE ON EXTRA CHORES

There is a tendency for clients, "since the consultant is here anyway," to load on unexpected or unpleasant tasks. The consultant, perhaps uncomfortable saying no, may comply—but end up feeling resentful. If the consultant does say no, you the client may feel put off. Either way, the request places an extra burden on the consulting relationship.

The solution? Raise the issue of additional tasks in the context of a renegotiation of the original contract—to include additional compensation, of course.

DO WHAT YOU AGREED TO DO

If you promised to return the consultant's phone calls within twenty-four hours, or inform him or her promptly of decisions, make sure you keep your word. To do otherwise not only will hamper the project, it will damage your relationship with the consultant.

A SPECIAL MESSAGE TO THE LIAISON PERSON

How do you know if you are the liaison person? Regardless of your title, if someone in your organization has brought in a consultant, and you are charged with managing, coordinating, or supporting the consultant's efforts, you are in the liaison role.

Here are some ways you can be most effective in this role:

- **Make sure you and your boss have a clear understanding of your respective roles regarding the consultant.** Who will hold progress meetings? Who will approve the project? And so on. Determine the authority you have. For example, can you authorize expenditures, or issue checks for project-related expenses?

- **Do your own contracting with the consultant.** Clarify your respective roles, and what you each need, want, or expect from the other. Perhaps the consultant will want you to schedule meetings for him or her. You may want the consultant to let you know if the project timetable starts to slip. Such expectations must be raised and dealt with.

- **Be alert for feelings of intimidation.** You may be reluctant to be assertive with an expert in your field. Suppose you're a project manager in a research and development group, and the consultant your boss hires is head of computer sciences at a major university. It may be difficult for you to push this consultant on slipping schedules or failures to keep you informed.

What should you do? Your ability to confront the consultant will depend to a great extent on how thoroughly you handled the contracting described in Section VI. If at your initial meeting you said something like, "Look, here's what the company expects from you, and part of my job is to let you know when that's not happening," your job will be much easier later. The failure of a consultant to meet stated expectations must be addressed head on.

MONITORING PROGRESS

Once a consulting project is under way, you (or your project manager or liaison person) will want to monitor progress on a regular basis. This will usually take the form of progress meetings with the consultant periodically—say, once a month—or as project milestones are reached.

Expect change. It's probably the one thing you can count on. Conditions will change, delays will occur, and refinements or improvements to the project will emerge.

Here are the key items to cover at your progress meetings:

☐ **Progress on the project.** What has been achieved, what hasn't, and how does this compare with the work plan as defined in the contract?

☐ **Obstacles that interefere with progress.** What's in the way, and what additional assistance does the consultant need from you or your people?

☐ **New or unforseen developments.** What changes in the organization or the external environment have occurred, or are anticipated, that will affect the project?

☐ **Adjustments to work plan or fees.** What revisions might need to be made to tasks, schedules, target dates, or fees? Any such updating should be confirmed in writing, signed by both parties, and filed with the original contract.

☐ **Preliminary findings.** What has the consultant observed or concluded so far? Be open to new ideas. As outsiders, consultants often have a fresh perspective on situations, and are willing to tell you things your staff may not.

MAINTAINING A PRODUCTIVE RELATIONSHIP

A productive relationship between you and the consultant will help move the project along. A poor relationship can delay or even derail it. Like most other relationships, this one requires attention. The key is to maintain a dialogue between you and the consultant—not just about the project, but also about your relationship.

Here are some suggestions to help you maintain a constructive working relationship with the consultant:

- **Voice your concerns—even minor ones.** A common error is to sit on minor annoyances or failed expectations because you feel they're too petty to mention. Don't let these build to the point where the consulting relationship is damaged. Instead, agree in advance that each of you will raise issues or concerns as they come up, no matter how minor.

- **Structure your progress meetings to include relationship issues as well as progress issues.** The question to ask is, *"How are we doing with each other?"* Raising this question takes courage. Most of us aren't comfortable being that direct—especially with someone we don't know that well. But the payoffs can be significant. First, there will be opportunities to give the consultant feedback in time for him or her to take corrective action. Second, you may find out what you do that contributes to and detracts from this relationship—and perhaps to other relationships as well. But there can be important side benefits that go well beyond the consulting project.

- **Give the consultant feedback—both positive and negative.** Report what is going well, and where needs or expectations aren't being met. Perhaps the consultant is not checking in often enough, or is brusque with your assistant on the phone. Tell the consultant immediately; it will only get more difficult with time.

- **Ask the consultant for feedback.** Working with a consultant provides a unique opportunity to learn about yourself and your management style. How you deal with the consultant—especially in difficult or stressful situations—is a reflection of how you deal with employees. Your employees won't always tell you the truth—at least not the full truth, but many consultants will, particularly those with strong interpersonal skills. So ask for feedback.

WHEN THINGS GO WRONG

Things **will** go wrong, despite your and the consultant's best intentions—even if you follow all the advice in this book.

You can, of course, foresee some major glitches and lessen their severity. Frequent progress meetings will provide you with an early warning system that alerts you to possible dangers ahead. Use these meetings to make corrections to the consultant's work plan, approach, or tactics.

Suppose you've done all that, and you still come up with a major problem. Here are the possibilities to consider:

1. **Evaluate whether the original timetable or goals were realistic.** If not, adjust the contract accordingly.

2. **Evaluate whether the situation has changed.** Even if the original goals and timetables were realistic at the time, the situation—either externally or within the company—may have changed enough to make the initial targets no longer appropriate. In this case, you need to reevaluate the project to decide whether to stop it temporarily, stop it permanently, continue with adjusted targets, or shift to a new or different objective.

   For example, suppose you hired a consultant to develop and install a revised accounting system. The project has slowed down because the internal people whose input is required are tied up dealing with a possible merger. In this case, it might be best to put the project on hold, in case the merger goes through, and your merger partner already has a more suitable accounting system.

WHEN THINGS GO WRONG
(Continued)

3. **Evaluate whether the consultant is performing poorly or has misrepresented his or her qualifications.** Making such a determination can be difficult, especially if the project is technical in nature and you're not technically trained. In this case, consider getting a second opinion from another technical consultant. (See the box on page 41, ''When you're hiring a technical consultant,'' for possible sources of evaluator consultants.) Of course, you'll need to be candid with your original consultant about your concerns, and the evaluation you plan to make. You may get some defensiveness, but don't let that stop you. You have a right to have your concerns checked out.

If the consultant has misrepresented qualifications or competencies, or the consultant's performance is unacceptable with no promise of improvement, the solution is simple: terminate the consultant. You should have a provision in your contract that covers this situation. Typically, you may need to give thirty days notice, and prorate the fee to cover the period the consultant worked. If your contract had a penalty clause, which reduces the consultant's fees for late delivery or nondelivery of the ''product,'' this may apply as well.

If the consultant's performance is poor, but not poor enough to warrant immediate termination, treat the situation much as you would a performance problem with an employee. That is, meet with the consultant to review the situation. Discuss the problem openly, and define the areas where performance falls short of expectations. Get the consultant's ideas on what he or she can do to improve the situation. Agree on the actions the consultant will take, and on any support you or your people will provide. Define the results you expect, and by when. Put all this in writing, and give it to the consultant. Meet again on the specified date to reevaluate the situation, and decide then whether to continue the project or terminate the relationship.

SECTION VIII
EVALUATING THE
CONSULTATION

Ideally, evaluation is an ongoing process. If you established interim milestones in your contracting with the consultant, and if you monitored these at periodic progress meetings, there should be no surprises at the end of the project. If and when the project goes off course, or schedules slip, you have the opportunity to give feedback, make adjustments, or renegotiate with the consultant.

The final evaluation is done after the project has ended. If you did a good job of contracting with the consultant, you will have agreed on what is to be different at the completion of the project (the deliverable or "product"), and how that is to be measured. After the project, you collect the necessary information and compare the achieved results against the target.

END-OF-PROJECT EVALUATION

Even if you've been monitoring progress along the way, there are several reasons why a formal evaluation at the end of the project makes sense:

1. **A postproject evaluation can give you and the consultant a sense of completion.** It gives you a chance to tie together any loose ends and create a feeling of closure.

2. **You may not have given adequate attention to setting milestones and monitoring progress.** Perfection is hard to achieve. The urgencies of managing an operation may have prevented you from monitoring the project as closely as you would like. You may need the end-of-project evaluation to know where you stand on the project, and with the consultant.

3. **There may be more work to do.** You may have achieved your objectives, but upon evaluating the project you may discover that follow-up work needs to be done. You may even find that there is a logical next step that wasn't anticipated at the start of the project. For example: you brought someone in to revamp your payroll system; the project went so smoothly that you now see where the consultant could be helpful with other systems' problems.

4. **It may be useful to assess the consultant's performance.** If you're with a large company, and the same consultant may be a candidate for other projects in other units, your evaluation can help determine whether the consultant should be hired again. (In some companies, formal written evaluations are performed after each project, and are available for review by those seeking consulting services.)

5. **There may be learnings for you.** Ultimately, the responsibility for whether a consulting project meets its goals rests with you, the client. Whatever the degree of success, by examining your contributions you can do better next time. For example, you may learn that you didn't check references carefully enough, weren't clear about the results you wanted, or moved too slowly in letting the consultant know when things weren't going well.

The evaluation at the end of the project consists of two major parts:

1. Gathering relevant information

2. Holding a meeting with the consultant

GATHERING INFORMATION

The information to collect includes:

- The ''before'' and ''after'' measurements on whatever the project was intended to change (for example, a specified increase in sales or in productivity).

- Any subjective reactions you or your people have about the consultant or the project (for example, bruised feelings, or resistance to the intended change).

- Your assessment of the consultant's performance: what the consultant did well, and what he or she could have done better. To assist you in doing the assessment of the consultant, use a sheet of paper with a line down the middle like this:

DID WELL	COULD HAVE DONE BETTER

THE EVALUATION MEETING

The meeting itself should provide for open and frank discussion of all relevant project areas. **Give the consultant advance notice of the meeting, and what you expect to cover.** Following is a possible agenda for the final evaluation meeting, along with explanatory comments after each agenda item.

1. Statement of Purpose

It's helpful to start **any** meeting with a review of the purpose of the meeting, no matter how obvious this may seem. This ensures a common understanding of why the meeting is being held. It also allows each party to state any additional needs they may have. For example, while the purpose of the meeting may be to evaluate the consulting project, the consultant may also want to address the issue of follow-up work.

2. Review of Project Objectives

In order to evaluate the project, you need to compare the results of the project against the project objectives—the original objectives as specified in your contract, or as revised at later meetings. So start the evaluation by making sure you and the consultant agree on what you were aiming for.

3. Consultant's Evaluation of the Project

Most consultants know very well what went well and what didn't. By first asking for the consultant's own evaluation of the project, you will minimize defensiveness. Also, if giving negative feedback is difficult for you, you may not have to say much if the consultant says it first.

4. Client's Evaluation of the Project

Now is the time to give your own candid assessment of how the project went. Don't hold back in an effort to be kind. Consultant's deserve honest feedback. And you have a right to give it.

5. Discussion of Differences in Perception

You and the consultant may see things differently. You can both benefit from an exchange of views.

6. Evaluation of the Relationship

It's important to evaluate how you and the consultant worked together. As with the project evaluation, you may want to start with the consultant's view, then yours, and follow with a discussion of the similarities and differences.

This can also be the opportunity for you to ask the consultant for feedback. What did you do that helped the consultant or the project? What did you do that got in the way? If the consultant is reluctant to respond with any negative information, try ''priming the pump'' by first stating your own self-assessment.

7. Discussion of Next Steps

Where do you go from here? This is the time to look at any unfinished project business, to consider an expansion or extension of the original contract, or to discuss any new or different projects you may be considering. For example, if the initial project called for a recommendation only, you may want to explore involving the consultant in the implementation phase.

WHAT HAVE I LEARNED

The last part of the evaluation is your personal assessment. What did you learn about yourself, or about managing consultants? How can you do things differently or better next time? You may find that you did a number of things very well—perhaps better than you expected. You may also find that there are some areas where you may want to improve your client skills, or change your customary ways of doing things. Finally, by exploring your role in the project, you may develop some self-awareness that can be helpful in other areas of your work and personal life.

Use the self-evaluation form on the next page to list what you did well and what you could have done better in each phase of the consulting process. For a fuller explanation of the phases, see ''The Consulting Process'' in Section I, or the appropriate individual section.

After you've completed the self-evaluation, use the Action Planning Guide on page 76 to apply what you've learned to your next consulting project.

SELF-EVALUATION AFTER THE PROJECT

PHASE	DID WELL	COULD HAVE DONE BETTER
1. Identifying the need	☐	☐
2. Deciding to hire	☐	☐
3. Defining a project objectives	☐	☐
4. Defining consultant criteria	☐	☐
5. Generating candidates	☐	☐
6. Choosing the consultant	☐	☐
7. Contracting with the consultant	☐	☐
8. Managing the relationship	☐	☐
9. Receiving the product or service	☐	☐
10. Evaluating the project and the relationship	☐	☐

ACTION PLANNING GUIDE

1. My current skills are most effective in the following areas:

   _____

   _____

   _____

2. I want to improve my client skills or do things differently next time in the following areas:

   _____

   _____

   _____

3. I've learned the following about my style or approach to managing consultants and consulting projects:

   _____

   _____

   _____

4. The following people or resources can help me improve my skills:

   _____

   _____

   _____

5. Here are my action steps, with specific timetables, to improve my client skills:

   _____

   _____

   _____

   _____

   _____

   _____

   _____

Quantity	Title	Code #	Price	Amount
	MANAGEMENT TRAINING			
	Self-Managing Teams	00-0	$7.95	
	Delegating for Results	008-6	$7.95	
	Successful Negotiation — Revised	09-2	$7.95	
	Increasing Employee Productivity	10-8	$7.95	
	Personal Performance Contracts — Revised	12-2	$7.95	
	Team Building — Revised	16-5	$7.95	
	Effective Meeting Skills	33-5	$7.95	
	An Honest Day's Work: Motivating Employees	39-4	$7.95	
	Managing Disagreement Constructively	41-6	$7.95	
	Learning To Lead	43-4	$7.95	
	The Fifty-Minute Supervisor — 2/e	58-0	$7.95	
	Leadership Skills for Women	62-9	$7.95	
	Coaching & Counseling	68-8	$7.95	
	Ethics in Business	69-6	$7.95	~
	Understanding Organizational Change	71-8	$7.95	
	Project Management	75-0	$7.95	
	Risk Taking	076-9	$7.95	
	Managing Organizational Change	80-7	$7.95	
	Working Together in a Multi-Cultural Organization	85-8	$7.95	
	Selecting And Working With Consultants	87-4	$7.95	
	Empowerment	096-5	$7.95	
	Managing for Commitment	099-X	$7.95	
	Rate Your Skills as a Manager	101-5	$7.95	
	PERSONNEL/HUMAN RESOURCES			
	Your First Thirty Days: A Professional Image in a New Job	003-5	$7.95	
	Office Management: A Guide to Productivity	005-1	$7.95	~
	Men and Women: Partners at Work	009-4	$7.95	
	Effective Performance Appraisals — Revised	11-4	$7.95	
	Quality Interviewing — Revised	13-0	$7.95	
	Personal Counseling	14-9	$7.95	
	Giving and Receiving Criticism	023-X	$7.95	
	Attacking Absenteeism	042-6	$7.95	
	New Employee Orientation	46-7	$7.95	
	Professional Excellence for Secretaries	52-1	$7.95	
	Guide to Affirmative Action	54-8	$7.95	
	Writing a Human Resources Manual	70-X	$7.95	
	Downsizing Without Disaster	081-7	$7.95	
	Winning at Human Relations	86-6	$7.95	
	High Performance Hiring	088-4	$7.95	
	COMMUNICATIONS			
	Technical Writing in the Corporate World	004-3	$7.95	
	Effective Presentation Skills	24-6	$7.95	
	Better Business Writing — Revised	25-4	$7.95	~

Quantity	Title	Code #	Price	Amount
	COMMUNICATIONS (continued)			
	The Business of Listening	34-3	$7.95	
	Writing Fitness	35-1	$7.95	
	The Art of Communicating	45-9	$7.95	
	Technical Presentation Skills	55-6	$7.95	
	Making Humor Work	61-0	$7.95	
	50 One Minute Tips to Better Communication	071-X	$7.95	
	Speed-Reading in Business	78-5	$7.95	
	Influencing Others	84-X	$7.95	
	PERSONAL IMPROVEMENT			
	Attitude: Your Most Priceless Possession — Revised	011-6	$7.95	—
	Personal Time Management	22-X	$7.95	
	Successful Self-Management	26-2	$7.95	
	Business Etiquette And Professionalism	32-9	$7.95	↲
	Balancing Home & Career — Revised	35-3	$7.95	
	Developing Positive Assertiveness	38-6	$7.95	
	The Telephone and Time Management	53-X	$7.95	
	Memory Skills in Business	56-4	$7.95	
	Developing Self-Esteem	66-1	$7.95	
	Managing Personal Change	74-2	$7.95	
	Finding Your Purpose	072-8	$7.95	
	Concentration!	073-6	$7.95	
	Plan Your Work/Work Your Plan!	078-7	$7.95	
	Stop Procrastinating: Get To Work!	88-2	$7.95	
	12 Steps to Self-Improvement	102-3	$7.95	↳
	CREATIVITY			
	Systematic Problem Solving & Decision Making	63-7	$7.95	
	Creativity in Business	67-X	$7.95	
	Intuitive Decision Making	098-1	$7.95	
	TRAINING			
	Training Managers to Train	43-2	$7.95	
	Visual Aids in Business	77-7	$7.95	
	Developing Instructional Design	076-0	$7.95	
	Training Methods That Work	082-5	$7.95	
	WELLNESS			
	Mental Fitness: A Guide to Emotional Health	15-7	$7.95	
	Wellness in the Workplace	020-5	$7.95	
	Personal Wellness	21-3	$7.95	
	Preventing Job Burnout	23-8	$7.95	
	Job Performance and Chemical Dependency	27-0	$7.95	
	Overcoming Anxiety	29-9	$7.95	
	Productivity at the Workstation	41-8	$7.95	
	Healthy Strategies for Working Women	079-5	$7.95	
	CUSTOMER SERVICE/SALES TRAINING			
	Sales Training Basics — Revised	02-5	$7.95	
	Restaurant Server's Guide — Revised	08-4	$7.95	
	Effective Sales Management	31-0	$7.95	

Quantity	Title	Code #	Price	Amount
	CUSTOMER SERVICE/SALES TRAINING (continued)			
	Professional Selling	42-4	$7.95	
	Telemarketing Basics	60-2	$7.95	
	Telephone Courtesy & Customer Service — Revised	64-7	$7.95	
	Calming Upset Customers	65-3	$7.95	
	Quality at Work	72-6	$7.95	
	Managing Quality Customer Service	83-1	$7.95	
	Customer Satisfaction — Revised	84-1	$7.95	
	Quality Customer Service — Revised	95-5	$7.95	
	SMALL BUSINESS/FINANCIAL PLANNING			
	Consulting for Success	006-X	$7.95	
	Understanding Financial Statements	22-1	$7.95	
	Marketing Your Consulting or Professional Services	40-8	$7.95	
	Starting Your New Business	44-0	$7.95	
	Direct Mail Magic	075-2	$7.95	
	Credits & Collections	080-9	$7.95	
	Publicity Power	82-3	$7.95	
	Writing & Implementing Your Marketing Plan	083-3	$7.95	
	Personal Financial Fitness — Revised	89-0	$7.95	
	Financial Planning With Employee Benefits	90-4	$7.95	
	ADULT LITERACY/BASIC LEARNING			
	Returning to Learning: Getting Your G.E.D.	02-7	$7.95	
	Study Skills Strategies — Revised	05-X	$7.95	
	The College Experience	07-8	$7.95	
	Basic Business Math	24-8	$7.95	
	Becoming an Effective Tutor	28-0	$7.95	
	Reading Improvement	086-8	$7.95	
	Introduction to Microcomputers	087-6	$7.95	
	Clear Writing	094-9	$7.95	
	Building Blocks of Business Writing	095-7	$7.95	
	Language, Customs & Protocol	097-3	$7.95	
	CAREER BUILDING			
	Career Discovery	07-6	$7.95	
	Effective Networking	30-2	$7.95	
	Preparing for Your Interview	33-7	$7.95	
	Plan B: Protecting Your Career	48-3	$7.95	
	I Got The Job!	59-9	$7.95	
	Job Search That Works	105-8	$7.95	

NOTE: ORDERS TOTALING LESS THAN $25.00 MUST BE PREPAID

	Amount
Total Books	
Less Discount	
Total	
California Tax (California residents add 7%)	
Shipping	.
TOTAL	

☐ Please send me a free Video Catalog.   ☐ Please add my name to your mailing list.

 ☐ Mastercard   VISA ☐ VISA   AMERICAN EXPRESS ☐ AMEX   Exp. Date _____

Account No. _____   Name (as appears on card) _____

Ship to: _____   Bill to: _____

_____   _____

_____   _____

_____   _____

Phone number: _____   P.O. #: _____

All orders of less than $25.00 must be prepaid. Bill to orders require a company P.O.#. For more information, call (415) 949-4888 or FAX (415) 949-1610.